LIVING FROM HERE

Bruce McConnell

LIVING FROM HERE
Poems 1968-2018

Anvil Press
Oakland

Three of these appeared in *First Poems, 1967-1970*

Acknowledgement

I feel deep gratitude to the many friends and loves who made it possible for these words to come from my heart onto the page, and especially dear Margaret.

July 2018

Cover Art: Christina Reynolds
Design Advice: Allen Levin

ISBN: 978-1-7325805-1-0

Printed in the United States of America

You don't *never* let go of the thread.

– with deep respect for
William Stafford
"The Way It Is"

CONTENTS

IN THE WORLD

IN FINE COMPANY

Old Growth Forest

In the west are rare places, precious
In abiding life. The mutable
Thrives amid thrust up brashness.
Life calls life – in the osprey's flight
Up river, in the firs' green moss
Deep in the shaded woods, in the glinting
Owl's eyes, in the hearth
Of old friendships rekindled, warm.

On the hills, in castles modest,
Built by careful hands, live the men,
Seasoned with grace and humor, the women,
Ripening in beauty and wisdom,
The lusts and dreams of youth
Beckoning, finding fullness.
In this land, waves break over me,
Unexpected streaming, memory –

The eucalyptus sweet perfume, the tang
Of marionberries, the jay's flap,
The junco's flitting, trill. I am light.
An old wing of the house has opened up.
The light streams in, the fresh air. We shake out
The old tablecloths and set the table.
Old love and new sprouts, a fertile tangle
Bears sweet community, forest and heart.

What Does Love Look Like?

Unexpected thoughtfulness.
Patience, unreserved.
An unnecessary smile.
Elation unrestrainable.

Listening well.
Creating sanctuary
Without judgment.
Holding, tenderly.

Exercised restraint.
Steadfast commitment.
The courage of sacrifice.
Cherishing the sacred.

At every turn, beloved,
Your face reappears, your
Voice echoes, your reflections
Bedazzle. Whenever, I tune in,

I am lost. I am complete.

Sunset at Solstice

The shortest day is over.
Tomorrow the cycle of
Renewal begins again.
Yet the weather will be cold
For several months. Won't you
Join me in the days ahead,
Finding our ways together?

And separately, for both are
Needed to survive, to thrive.
Others may come along this
Way with us. May we prepare
To welcome them from our own
Strength, bring their lights and darkness
Into this warm place of love.

For healing will be needed
In the days ahead. This work,
Creating a new order,
Is not for the faint of heart.
In the meantime, on this night,
Let us curl up by the fire
Enjoy the festival of light.

On Garlic

for my brother

When I crush and peel garlic I think of you,
Perhaps from the night we made
Chicken cacciatore, something
We did in hunter's style.
In your Yorkville basement kitchen.

Back home, tonight's garlic finds company
With peppers, okra, squash, tomatoes:
Locals of a southern city.
That night I left before dessert;
The cabbie, botching the turn,
Toured around Penn Station.

Our wives report you finished
All the chicken, showing a preacher's
Sunday appetite, while I, facing north,
Rode south on clattering rails.

Solitude in travel is the rule.
That night, though, I rode
With boon companion,
The sweet scent
Lingering on my fingertips.

October Moon

for my father

Strains of a high school song
Our boys will shine
Come to the mind tonight
From a long time.

Grown in a southern town
Toughened in fire
The old man walks down with me,
All down the line.

Daily we work the row,
Column and page,
Listen to tone of speech,
Options arrayed.

Laden by works of men
Contending strong,
Afloat in the earthy flood,
We move along.

Two years he's in the grave,
Thirty-nine am I,
Three score those high school days,
Under the sky.

Unwind Old Habits

Clean the house, discarding what no longer
Serves, is worn out, out of style, for which
There is no room, or just stopped being fun.
Furniture, heirlooms, practical life tools
Jumbled together. Discernment first is
The ideal. Or ease it where it pinches.

Still, one must say goodbyes, with fondness for
Roles well-played . . . being a great seat for the
Soul, say, or having made life run smoothly
In the ways it has always run, the dear,
Old ways, time-tested, the quirks and flaws
Predictable. Change is a cruel mistress.

Which habits? Taking the dog out? Lighting
The supper candle? Not really. Sleeping
On one's side of the bed? Assuming Home
Is where one lays one's head? Keep the good. Be
Kind. In this sacred grove, only prune, do
Not fell. Cultivate for a long future.

Surrender to Love

We see it, that future, emerging from
Shadow, as through a darkened glass, beyond
Imagination rushing toward
Us at breakneck speed. We may choose: refuse,
Retreat, adapt, lean in. There is no do,
Only be, in love, for love, or, beauty.

Delicious intimacies, life's sweetest
Nectars, reveal their origins in heart's
Fires: ego, compassion, desire; fondness,
Affection; fantasy, or delusion;
Terror; and release. I have stopped trying
To figure it out. Or to explain it.

So what does that look like, in the crystal
Ball? How does it feel: like a rolling stone,
Or in communion, in community?
I want both. In full measure. The sacred
In the profane. I will walk in your shoes,
Invite you into mine. That love may teach us.

In a Taxi to LaGuardia

Sometimes the morning
Is so entirely beautiful
I can barely look, the blood orange sun
Turning the steam clouds purple,
The icy sparkle off warming snow.

I fall back, into last night's
Half full waxing moon, your
Own dear eyes, clear, twinkling.

What's New

Because of you, life is new.

—Carlos Santana

A tall, slender creature roams my brain,
Opening the windows. A year of this,
Salt breeze in my nostrils on waking,
Fog horns entering my sleep,
I am restless. My live bones
Strain, my joints in pain connect.

Books tumble from the shelf spilling ideas,
Seeds of a viney bramble, habitat
To new thought. My pulse speeds. Fair eyes
Sparkle, feed me across the table.
A word from you gets me through a whole day.

Old ways loved, worn past perfection and patched,
Suffer, cry to be restored. Tears rise
As the past crumbles. Once more
Try to make it work.

Soft words in the distance lift my heart;
Commitment steels my own. For all this
I am grateful.

The Wheel

Turning once more to letting go
Of you, I fall away, tender,
Stewed meat exposing bone. The sweet
Portion we, deep in love, prepared
Standing in our kitchens under
Many moons, will soon be served, in
Concert with traditional fare.

Perhaps we knew it would be like
This, the most succulent dish is
Often found among contorni,
Leaving a longing for more.
Surrender, beautiful hearts, lost
Once, forever in each other,
Lost anew, embracing the world.

Oma

For you these days I am singing and
Being happy, even inside.
My life is patterned in a crystal
Dewdrop, on a golden butterfly.
Blessings, blessings on thee,
Rusty lady, anchor
In the half-lit early sea.

Return

These are three friends. There is creation: here,
This smooth, flat, wave-worked stone, the frail threads
Between. Of us there will remain small things
Or even words. Men have spent all of time
In tireless reading of each other's lines:
The endless pounding on the shores tonight;
Then gently at our backs the morning, light.

Fine Company

We arrived by night, bags spilling
Onto your floor, happily
Crashing into each others'
Arms, and sleep.

In the morning the tide was in,
Feeding mud crabs and sand dollars,
Mixing families, disturbing
Chemistry.

Hearts intertwining, personal
Ecologies combined
For too few days, we cooked, rode,
Read, walked, talked.

Ideas, feelings, little
Histories, great passages,
Roads, woods, moon, theater:
Made feast days.

Now the sea is gone
Back to its own place, as we
Remember sweetly, eyes bright,
Glistening.

River of Love

Some years ago, after seasons of rain,
A chunk of shoreline crumbled. No more the
Sheltered cove where our boats had tied, shady
And green in all weathers. Now, the current.
Chaos.

Of necessity we each relearned
Piloting and navigation, safety,
And the purposes of various knots.
We are good enough to ply the torrents,
Avoid the whirlpools, be warm in the storm.
Progress.

We are strong enough to tie up nearby,
To take some days, stretch out our souls, enjoy
The swells, the calling of crow and heron
From the trees, the lights in each other's eyes.
Sunsets.

Calmer waters, treacherous rapids? Can
Another travel with me? We wrestle
Through divergent headings, make some way,
Powered by the thrum, community, and
Solitude.

Under and within us, without end,
The river runs, rolls on around the bend.
Whether up an icy creek, down thrilling
Fork or autumn rivulet, I chart you
Tenderly, sensing the course to our next
Meeting.

The stars and winds, ever my companions,
Remind me it is all one river. Our
Lovestream flows within it, mysterious,
Alive.

Coming Home

You stand waiting, as I wait,
Wait for our waitings' end.
You are my roof and my foundation.
You are my secret weapon
In the fray. Now soon beside me
In the flesh, your laugh live in my ears,
I'll find your sweetest mouth with mine,
Our lives resuming near.

Letting Go

What has been taught in these few years?
Love is not anyone's to own.

All we are given is as a gift:
Gratitude for living, and chances
To know and love another well.
Now, the grit to cultivate
Patience, compassion, courage fair;
Equanimity amidst deep conflict;
Humility and thankfulness for
What delicious forms and moments
The Universe may offer in its time
To such unworthy, blessèd pilgrims.

INSIDE

How Then, to Live from Here?

I surrender, again and
Somehow, finally — lost
To the abyss. Hallelujah.

First Priapus, then Thor
Has been admitted
To the Council fire.

They have come in
From the nether region,
Stinking of blood and shit.

Welcome, Dear Ones, come,
Take a load off. Thank you
For all you have done:

Over the years,
Toiling in obscurity,
Minding the Holy fires of Hell.

—

The Wise Old Man reports.
He is well. He is ready
To tell his story.

Since the earliest days,
He has lived in two worlds.
The veil now is pierced.

The lights shine through.
The division is ended.
The day has arrived

When he can sit
At the head of the circle
Because everyone is present.

Why, you might ask,
Admit these coarse fellows
To our civilized gathering?

The answer is the same
As the reason why the
Old Man loves them.

They simply do not give
A shit. Theirs is the
Terrible swift sword.

They have not been idle
These many years. They
Persevere, decide, act.

They hold space in all weather,
For equanimity, for justice,
For freedom, and for sacrifice.

They are not afraid of dying.
They are not going back.
Welcome, brothers. Welcome

Home: this place where
Everything is lost,
And there is peace.

Here will the Feminine tend your wounds,
The child run out before you,
The dog cherish your hand.

Here there is music and dance
And room for your stories and songs
Heard without judgment.

For you have had enough
With judgment. We have all
Had enough. There is no more time.

The watch fires of the world
Blaze anew in fear. Steadfast,
We shall not be moved,

Neither by fear of loss
Nor death, nor love. Abiding in you,
Beloved, in full measure.

Allelu.

Sending Upstream

In the swift current
Time is compressed:
Face ahead only.

Broken from my crowd –
Boatmen
Boisterous and green,
We'd shared headings
Across the swell.

Now I post letters
From remote landings:
Boat running well;
Stars favorable.
Pilot queasy,
Firm on the wheel.
Your last news
Burns in my heart.

Dreaming

Sometimes, eyes closed
the big screen dark
shadow-shapes
move.
three a.m.
deserted cobbles
shining with rain,
an iron-wheeled cart
bears a clutter of echoes
from yesterday, overtures
from tomorrow, tethered
forever
in this
moment.
Slowly shedding its
wearies, the body
begins to fall away,
dissolve, ooze out,
flatten into an
unboundaried expanse,
become sea water only the
orifices remaining
palpable, sentient, breathing
barely worth the effort.

Space complies, aligns,
conspires to bring the outside
in, noises integrate, the
click of a latch a pistol
someone's moan a warning
the tide at neap.

Finally, the observer
surrenders. I feel so alive
I can hardly sleep.

River Craft

on the White House staff, 1990s

Untethered in the current
Its level is as all boats.
The motor is engaged
Going where I'm going.

Service, an ideal:
Keep the president informed,
Reconcile divergent views,
Tell the legislature and the public,
Manage crisis. This is not direction,
It is what our little fleet is built for.

With the river, and experience,
The view changes. Around the bend
All manner of traffic can be seen
Plying the ports and inlets.

I'll shoot the stars or shoot the rapids
Before I take this all-weather tub
Into any place particular. It's the
Sailing and the company,
Keep me afloat.

Western

We seek that fair home on the range
Where the ungulates' lives so arrange
What pain grieves the heart
They turn over to art,
Finding beauty and sunsets deep orange.

These Long Nights

All winter I sleep
Badly, my weary heart
Waiting to bloom again.

Free Fall

Again. Only this
Time it feels like floating. All
The way down, inside.

Coming In

For a time it seemed as if the autumn
Had forgot its measured sequence, cast
Its goal aside, and I began to move
Again. The flow of sap, slow in the trees,
And then, just a slight wind among the leaves,
All, with the sun's slow ease, warming.

There was in this the certain promise, spring,
Which, ransomed by these winter days, betrays
Its fleeting truth. So, does the cold require
This old rekindling of the inside fires
And with the movement of the winter, waiting.

song of loneliness

friends gathered together
unconsummated gaiety
living in differences
trying this new day;

sparsely the trees stand,
howl winter wind
ancient within me
echo of Coyote.

Making Room

Born full tilt into a river flowing –
choking, blinded by sight – into a torrent's roar,
no chart to tell me of the torrent's going
no record of a passing here before.

—Ken Kesey

1

Ganesh he is not, yet bears fond
resemblance: rotund, jocose, a
mild air of menace. And power.

His origin story begins
not in India, but from within
the inner realm, tangled in
cross-wired threads of lineages
fighting through Asia, Europe,
the efflorescence of Saxons
and Sioux, cotton and sinew,
out of Kentucky and Kansas,
Arkansas and Saint Paul, flying
into China, and on, to the
crucible and cradle of
Washington, and
hence.

An elephant like this tends
toward ranging, hungry, a bit
reckless. And stubborn. Fit neither
for parlor nor paddock, it yearns
for living room, habitat.

2

Now we must proceed more slowly
idle the engines, make no wake,
heed this perilous stretch of water,
trust the currents to take us in.

Free falling can exhilarate:
Keep chute packed, at hand.
Even the hard landing teaches.
Christoph, preserve us.

3

I am not the elephant, just
an ordinary man within whom
this fine beast abides, doggedly,
alongside otter, eagle, salmon,
from the nine directions.
For you, now must be cobbled
accommodation suitable
to your great stature, prodigious
appetite, vital heart.

To fail to attempt this is
to die, that is, to suffer out
the remaining eras in stays,
irons or baleen it does not
matter.

4

Such rough talk summons the ancient Fear,
Gnawing at the bone of history.
Without life, it cannot exist.
It suffers me to regain the path.

5

Meanwhile, there's bigger game afoot!
How to make a difference? Align
at every level; chakra; tone;
modality; dimension; hue.

Every living thing.

6

For with you, delicious being,
can be tenderly uncovered
vast and sacred incarnations,
relaxation, exultation.
Such beauty, such oases,
whether brief or everlasting,
are the way points and the way.

7

It comes thus to provision
for life as we will come to know it.
There is no playbook. We have passed
the event horizon. We are
running headlong through an open field.

Guts, faith, stamina…trusted,
imaginative, resonant
circles: what more is needed?

Only your presence.

In Preparation

The high grass between forest and plain
has given way to open, rolling country
that extends in all directions.
I have been walking for days, happy in the
coolness of shade.
I dig shallow roots, feel hungry.

In emptiness, humble gifts appear: my tools,
my hands' skill, noises of birds, the wind's,
and within, the unwithering stillness,
all grown large again, as new. My age falls
away, stirring up old sadness. I wait.

Life, its sweet chain binding, draws me,
memory and hope dancing in a round.
Gladly I return, entering silently
the thickness of the woods, picking up
the daily rising and falling
of tools and hopes.
I sleep warm at my lover's side. Let me
share my gifts and keep them, against
brutality's painful hour,
when fear rules the trembling heart.

Raw Love (Amor Fati)

After coffee you can start from here.
Faint scents of bliss, and of destruction
Waft through the window, arouse. Almost
Fearless, you rise shivering, sail
Tenderly, boldly into your life.
It helps if you break clinch with yesterday,
Become lighter, more essential.

What happens next, what fusion with the
Day's ordinary, is so much less
Your choice than you were taught. All you can
Do, really, is try to keep your heart
Open, your mind curious, your soul
In awe. You fall in love with the world,
Into its rhythms. Your heartstrings sigh
In contentment. Life's exultation,
Its human pain, become your own. On
A good day those whom you must love, each
In their own way, laugh and weep with you.

At evening, there is time for reflection.
You fall back, rue your brokenness, review
The costs of living and who shall bear them
Into the night. Offer them up. Hone
Your craft. Vow to cultivate compassion.
Honor truth and kindness. Look ahead,
But do not think you are the Captain.

In The World

Emergence

Through grace, courage, persistence,
fortune, history, guile, and massive love
unmerited, and with plentiful helpers and
guides, this unsuspecting man has been
transported, released to plant and tend
great circles of blooming harmony!

My totem animals emerge from sky and
water, jungle and forest: bat, eagle, whale
and salmon, tiger, otter, raven, porcupine.
From the nine directions they surround me.
As one, among the sparking memes,
machines, we move.

In the tunnels of the Temple of Janus, light
and dark contend, connect in unexpected,
dissonant harmony. I seek possibilities
among obscured communities of service,
wary but optimistic, heeding the silent
coursing of the hourglass.

In some weathers, way can be made.

Pre-Dawn Jazz

Side-by-side three radio towers are
Blinking, each in its own cadence. Through the
Pane their orange-red lamps create stick figures
That remind me of 火, fire.

Sometimes they appear together,
But mostly as staggered pairs or
Solo, they dance, legs kicking high,
Arms spread in playful exuberance.

The planet drum sustains the beat
Across the separate frequencies,
Dissonances, harmonies
Flashing on the wet, black street.

Dawn Augury

Beijing

A vast parking lot stretches
Beyond my high window,
Holding only a man with a kite.
The bird soars higher, floats and flutters
Lazily, silent, belies its tether.
To the East, the air is clear.

Later, some men will come to fly
Drones; and from the West,
Coal smoke and Gobi sand.

When I look up from the page
They are gone.

The Mowing

*Thus far the Rome Plows have cleared an area
the size of Luxembourg.*

—Vietnam dispatch, 1972

The task is to make borders clear.
There is an end to cutting grass
To please the eye, mine and my neighbor's;
My lawn matches with his along the street.
In back, the blades seek the high grass,
The engine muffles, cuts it down.

My closeness to the farmer is
The Rome Plow, my harvest is sores
On the faces of the earth,
The blood on our hands. Line upon
Line fall in steady progress.
The clover heads do not resist.
The grass settles into place
In seasons, turning in pattern
To the boiling sun. Deep rooted,
Of ancient, bastard seed, weeds
Rise to disturb the order.

Abattoir: Four Words

at Prather Ranch

Respect: these fruits of earth and sun
Have been brought, innocent, into
This place. We bow to them: cycle
Of life, regenerate. All is
Used. Our humanity persists.
In the old days, first say a prayer.

Mastery: no wasted motion.
Keeping their tools sharp, these artists
Peel hide from the quick, a whole piece.
Likewise the soft sheath full of guts,
Large as a sack of potatoes,
Falls cleanly into its pan.

Cohesion: seven people move
In the tall room. One bleeds. Two wash
A now recumbent carcass as
One. Two tend to precious organs,
One painstakingly dissects a
Head. Silence. Slow, solemn folk dance.

Presence: a few thousand pounds of
Flesh, held in four great masses, hold
The attentions of all humans
Present. From the warm summer day
They are on their way to the chill
Room of aging. As we all are.

Early Morning

Today is West Virginia, rain again;
And this place, Grafton. On the river, fog
Muffles the motorcycle as I cross.
An Esso sign revolves against the sky's
Old grey. A man emerges, blowing on
His hands and, standing in the rain he lets
The orange tonic flow into the black
Gas tank. Like young girls sleeping, growing old
Who climb in pale clothes at midday, empty,
Out of boredom to the custard stand,
He is of us whose trust is in the road.

Rosscarbery, West Cork

Could be anywhere
Looking out
From some window onto
Some scene of the
World. In here, it's
The inner world speaks
Loud its certain coda,
Chorus simple.

Hew to that inner
Understanding, that
Curlew call, the
Shrill piping of plenty,
The heartbeat of the soul.
Only in this shall ye find
Salvation, you who carry
Without blame, or will,

The legacy of this land.

Marker

They left us names in steel
Against the quick neat frame
Of memory's appeal.
Like gems in light, or flames
They sparkle and conceal.

The Old Wound

Heartache of separation
man from man
clan upon clan
state against state:
adversary foe enemy devil
or simply not-of-mine, other.

People and evil
feed each other
from the heartache,
the original separation
from God, from Mom, from
Love, compounded over years,
generations, left unhealed.

Project for a Revolution

in St. Louis, 1970s

A People's Movement comes
into touch with what all
collectively know as secret.
It's not just Life no it is
the Other also,
me and you Hey – hey
you! Remember
what Mama used to say...
Don't count those chickens
before they hatch?
Well. It's just about
nobody here's made it,
and I mean economically,
emotionally <u>and</u> spiritually.
You got those one or two
percenters, here and there,
but the people as a whole
are strugglin'...
for Me, yeah, I Want, yeah.

If I take what I want
will what you want be left?
Not unless one of us is a saint.
And not being a saint,
I guess I want you and me
to share equally in the
benefits of our dear planet,

to enjoy equally the joys
of this home life, to share
equally in the tasks.
What I mean is let's help
each other look around
and see you, sister,
and you, brother, and you, friend.

Yeah, well I'll just doze off
here in my nightmare dream
of pretty colored fantasies
and float away. I guess I
can't hear you weeping,
I can't see you laughing
outside my self.

Let me know
if you read me, comrade,
and I'll step across the room
and hug you and share with you
a whole portion of earth's love
and we shall start over
as part of one body
one spirit one earth.

entering in

unsung relinquishing stretches
behind us, the sadness. is
following enough? – eye to the
light, the flow of seasons, open
vessel…. i speak of friends:
fresh folds crease the fabric here;
there's blindness, shielded light.
they walk stiffly, glutted
flies in a stifled air.
yet each fir alive is singing
hard needles in the place of hair.

this is the show. today, the future,
ah, clown, painfully dancing…
(glumly they sit, wasted, well-fed).
there, a thousand flowers bloom; there
dogs run: the ancient field,
the deep clear light. for too long
we have swum toward our destiny
like sperm. ever strangers, murderers.

i have a habit of erring.
we share near the edge of the
galaxy, passion-common ground,
this acquiescent worthy stage,
lone live child of a yellow sun.
equal with bear, pine and willow,
i am come visiting in human
settlements: leaf-like we reach
upon past reaching;
our roots, old,
hold. live only! build, heal!

Psalm

The old ways beckon. From within the flow,
trickles follow the land's lay, drawn to earth.
The land holds all the rain, shaping its course
in the valleys of its history.

A person's mask is etched in the clays
of his own land. He must make of it
what he will. Only this is hope.

A Friday

In my kitchen
Sun is setting.
Chopping figs
Coarsely, fondly:
Reflections on the
Spicy fragrance of the
Curry, complex,
Earthy, that
Is coming, that
Is
Life.

Colophon

The text was typeset in Microsoft Garamond, and
Stempel Garamond LT Standard from LinoType.

Anvil Press
Oakland

Made in the USA
San Bernardino, CA
17 December 2018